Revenge of the Grannies

Level 10 – White

Helpful Hints for Reading at Home

The graphemes (written letters) and phonemes (units of sound) used throughout this series are aligned with Letters and Sounds. This offers a consistent approach to learning whether reading at home or in the classroom.

HERE ARE SOME COMMON WORDS THAT YOUR CHILD MIGHT FIND TRICKY:

water	where	would	know	thought	through	couldn't
laughed	eyes	once	we're	school	can't	our

TOP TIPS FOR HELPING YOUR CHILD TO READ:

- Encourage your child to read aloud as well as silently to themselves.
- Allow your child time to absorb the text and make comments.
- Ask simple questions about the text to assess understanding.
- Encourage your child to clarify the meaning of new vocabulary.

This book focuses on developing independence, fluency and comprehension. It is a white level 10 book band.

WEST SUSSEX LIBRARY SERVICE	
202079500	
Askews & Holts	06-Sep-2021
JF BEG	

Revenge of the Grannies

Written by
Robin Twiddy

Illustrated by
Rosie Groom

Grannies – they are nice and sweet, and they give you treats, right? But don't cross them, I can tell you that much. I have seen what happens if you do. Trust me, they are sweet until they have a reason to fight. Then the teeth come out.

Literally.

It was the summer holidays and I was looking forward to spending a week with Gran. She knows all sorts of things, lets me have treats that Mum and Dad won't and tells me stories from the old days. Gran is pretty great!

But when I arrived at her house, something was different. She wasn't in her usual cheery mood. She was pacing up and down the hallway, muttering under her breath.
"Hi, Gran," I said, waving.
"Oh yes, hi Doyle," she replied. "Just put your stuff in the spare room."
I put my things away and said goodbye to Mum.

"What are the plans for the week, Gran?" I asked hopefully. "Are we going to watch old war movies? Or look at pictures from the time that you explored the Sahara?"

That's the thing about old people, we forget that they were once young people.

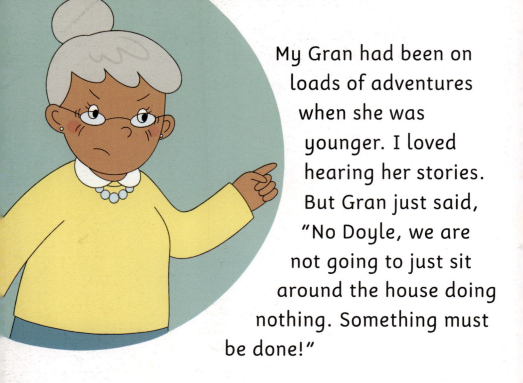

My Gran had been on loads of adventures when she was younger. I loved hearing her stories. But Gran just said, "No Doyle, we are not going to just sit around the house doing nothing. Something must be done!"

I had no idea what she was going on about.

"And I am the one who is going to do it," she continued.
"Do what, Gran?" I asked.
"Get revenge!" she said, raising a fist into the air. She stormed off to her closet and started rummaging through her old things.
"It must be here," she muttered to herself.
Things flew out of the closet over her shoulders.

"Ah ha," she shouted triumphantly, as she pulled an ancient leather jacket out and dusted it off. "Did I ever tell you about the time I was in a biker gang?" she said, looking dreamily at the jacket. It was covered in patches with funny names and phrases on them, such as 'Chopper' and 'Ride Till You Can't'. There was even a huge one on the back that had a big flaming skull on it.

"What's going on?" I asked.
"I told you," she said. "I am getting revenge, and you're going to help me." She kicked open the garage door and tossed me a black motorcycle helmet. "You're going to need this," said Gran, before she strode into the garage.

Inside the garage, she walked to a dark corner and grabbed hold of a sheet. She whipped it off, into the air. The sheet drifted to the floor behind her. Where it had been, stood a huge black motorcycle with flames running down each side.

"Wow," I heard myself say out loud.

"Get on, then," said Gran.
"Where are we going?" I said, climbing onto the bike and gripping Gran tightly around the waist.
"To get the gang back together," she said, starting the bike with a big kick.
Then we were out on the open road roaring along at high speeds. The bike's engine was thundering away underneath us.

We pulled up next to a sign that read 'Creaky Knees Retirement Home'.
"This is the place," she said, hanging her helmet on the handle of the bike. I still didn't know what we were doing there but by the time that I had got off the bike, Gran was hammering on the front door with her fist.

"Hello, miss," said the man who answered the door. "What can I do for you? Are you here to visit someone?" Gran pushed a toffee in his mouth and forced her way through the door. "I'm getting the gang back together," she shouted as she marched down the hall. "Sorry, mister," I said. "She's on a mission – a mission for revenge."
I ran after her.

"They'll be in here," Gran said, opening a large set of doors to reveal a bingo hall.
"Two fat ladies..." the bingo caller said into his microphone. Before he knew what was happening, Gran was next to him, toffee in hand. Pop! The toffee was now in his mouth.
"Mumble, mumble, squelch," said the bingo caller. His mouth was too full of toffee to speak.

Gran grabbed the microphone and turned to the hall of old people waiting for the next number in the game.

Gran stared at them for a long time. Then she spoke. She was like one of those generals from the old war movies we watched together, giving the big speech to inspire the troops.

"They think we are old," she said. "They think we are stupid. They think we won't notice. Well I did! I noticed!" she said. "They think we will just sit back and accept it. We won't!" Gran was pacing back and forth across the stage. Nothing could stop her now.

"Accept what?" came a voice from the crowd. "They are going to bulldoze Madison Park," Gran said. "They are going to build a big multistorey car park there!"
"But that's where I met my Burt," the same voice from the crowd said.
"And that's where I go to feed the ducks!" said another.

"Doris, Mildred, Gertie, Nora, have you still got your bikes?" Gran asked.

"You bet," one of the ladies said.

"Well go and get them, girls. Because today, the Rose Ladies ride again!" Gran shouted.

"The rest of you, meet us at the park as soon as you can."

"The Rose Ladies?" I asked.

"That's what our gang was called," Gran said while offering me a toffee.

"Droopy drawers, 44," the bingo caller said, having finally won the battle with the toffee.

We waited outside on Gran's bike. I heard the Rose Ladies coming before I saw them. The four bikes made quite a racket, but over the top of the din I could hear the Rose Ladies whooping and hollering. They were a real wild bunch.

"Right ladies, let's ride!" shouted Gran over the revving engines of the Rose Ladies. Then we were off, cruising through the normally quiet streets of town. We must have been quite a sight, five old ladies in leather jackets and a boy of nine zooming through the streets on huge motorcycles.

When we arrived at the park, the bulldozers were already there. It looked like they were about to get started. Gran skidded her bike to a stop on the gravel, sending a shower of stones raining down on a sleeping workman.

"Right!" Gran said through gritted teeth. She walked furiously towards the startled workman. I didn't know a walk could be furious until I saw her walk.

"Eh, uh... what's going on?" said the workman. He brushed gravel off of his chest and looked up at the sky with a suspicious eye, as if expecting more to fall on him.

Gran poked the workman in the centre of his chest. He stumbled back a step.
"Who's in charge around here?" Gran said. She poked him again and the man stumbled back another step.

"Hey," said the workman as he received another prod to the chest. "Ow! Alright, alright, Mr Trank is over there," he said, pointing to a well-dressed man in a hard hat. Gran spun on her heels and headed in the direction the finger had pointed in. The other Rose Ladies were now behind her. Poor Mr Trank didn't know what was coming his way.

"You!" growled Gran. "You are going to pack away all your tools, start up the engines on those trucks and bulldozers and drive away from our park!"

"Well, madam," Mr. Trank said. "I'm afraid we can't do that. We are about to start work on this building site. Why don't you and your lovely friends go to the bingo or something."

"We just came from there!" said Doris. Gran gave Doris a hard look then turned back to Mr. Trank. "We are not going back to the bingo until you have agreed to leave the park and never come back!"

"We can't do tha—" began Mr. Trank, when he was interrupted by a hissing sound.

He looked over Gran's shoulder at Nora, who was removing a knitting needle from the tyre of a bulldozer that hissed loudly as it slowly let down.

"Hey!" shouted Mr. Trank. "They are expensive!"

Gran grabbed Mr. Trank by the jaw and pulled his face close to hers. She stared at his face for a long time.

"I know you," she said. "Little Tarquin Trank from up on the hill! I knew you when you were just a little boy, no older than my grandson. Do you still live in that big old house with the big gardens?"

"Yes, I do," said Tarquin Trank.
"Well, Tarquin," Gran said. "If you won't stop on your own then we will stop you."
Mr Trank looked around at the five old ladies and then at the twenty men who worked for him. He seemed to grow more confident.
"You and what army?" he said.

Tarquin's eyes widened. He was staring at something in the distance just over Gran's shoulder. It was an army – an army of old people riding mobility scooters over the hill and down the path towards the park.

"This army!" Gran said, stretching her arms out.

Gran got close to Tarquin again.
"If you take our park away, we will need to find somewhere else to go in the evenings. If I remember correctly, and I always do," said Gran, "that big house of yours has a lovely big garden with some nice benches and a beautiful pond."

Tarquin gulped.

"Maybe we will come and visit... EVERY SINGLE DAY!" Gran warned Mr Trank.

"All of you?" Mr Trank squeaked.

"All of us!" replied Gran.

"Right!" shouted Mr. Trank to the workmen. "Pack it up, the job's off. Let's get out of here!"

And just like that, they were gone. Suddenly a huge cheer rose up from the crowd of old people. They threw their flat caps and wigs in the air in celebration. Gran had won. The Rose Ladies had won! Revenge had been served!

The rest of my week with Gran was much calmer, but still great. I spent most of it in the park with the Rose ladies, hearing stories from the old days. That summer, I learned a lot of things, but most importantly I learned never to underestimate old people. Especially when they are out for revenge!

Revenge of the Grannies

1. What was Doyle's gran upset about?

2. What was Doyle's gran's gang called?

3. Which do you think is better for a town to have, a new carpark or a park?

4. How did Gran get the bingo caller to be quiet?

5. Have you ever felt as passionate as Gran felt about saving the park?

©2021 BookLife Publishing Ltd.
King's Lynn, Norfolk PE30 4LS

ISBN 978-1-83927-438-1

All rights reserved. Printed in Malaysia.
A catalogue record for this book is available from the British Library.

Revenge of the Grannies
Written by Robin Twiddy
Illustrated by Rosie Groom

An Introduction to BookLife Readers...

Our Readers have been specifically created in line with the London Institute of Education's approach to book banding and are phonetically decodable and ordered to support each phase of Letters and Sounds.

Each book has been created to provide the best possible reading and learning experience. Our aim is to share our love of books with children, providing both emerging readers and prolific page-turners with beautiful books that are guaranteed to provoke interest and learning, regardless of ability.

BOOK BAND GRADED using the Institute of Education's approach to levelling.

PHONETICALLY DECODABLE supporting each phase of Letters and Sounds.

EXERCISES AND QUESTIONS to offer reinforcement and to ascertain comprehension.

BEAUTIFULLY ILLUSTRATED to inspire and provoke engagement, providing a variety of styles for the reader to enjoy whilst reading through the series.

AUTHOR INSIGHT:
ROBIN TWIDDY

Robin Twiddy is one of BookLife Publishing's most creative and prolific editorial talents, who imbues all his copy with a sense of adventure and energy. Robin's Cambridge-based first class honours degree in psychosocial studies offers a unique viewpoint on factual information and allows him to relay information in a manner that readers of any age are guaranteed to retain. He also holds a certificate in Teaching in the Lifelong Sector, and a postgraduate certificate in Consumer Psychology.

A father of two, Robin has written over 70 titles for BookLife and specialises in conceptual, role-playing narratives which promote interaction with the reader and inspire even the most reluctant of readers to fully engage with his books.

This book focuses on developing independence, fluency and comprehension. It is a white level 10 book band.